STEAM ACROSS
THE PENNINES

CHRIS GEE

HALSGROVE

First published in Great Britain in 2011

British Library Cataloguing-in-Publication Data
A CIP record for this title is available from the British Library

ISBN 978 0 85710 059 7

HALSGROVE
Halsgrove House,
Ryelands Business Park,
Bagley Road, Wellington, Somerset TA21 9PZ
Tel: 01823 653777   Fax: 01823 216796
email: sales@halsgrove.com

Part of the Halsgrove group of companies.
Information on all Halsgrove titles is available at: www.halsgrove.com

Printed in Italy by Grafiche Flaminia

INTRODUCTION

The Pennine hills and mountains stretch from the Peak District in Derbyshire and Staffordshire, where limestone gives way to gritstone, across northern England through Lancashire, Yorkshire and Cumbria, almost to the border with Scotland. Separating north-western England from the North East, they are sometimes called the 'backbone of England' or the 'roof of England' and have long been a natural barrier to transport between east and west.

The Pennines include some of the first national parks – the Peak District and Yorkshire Dales – and some Areas of Outstanding Natural Beauty – such as Pendle Hill, the Forest of Bowland and the North Pennines. Geologically it also includes the West Pennine Moors and the Rossendale Fells. The popular conception is that the Pennines start at Edale at the start of the Pennine Way – a long distance footpath that runs through to the border with Scotland near Kirk Yetholm. However, in geological terms the Pennines are a mix of carboniferous limestone and millstone grit, their true beginning being in the area of the Roaches and Shutlingsloe near Macclesfield.

Although there are few significant towns on the higher ground, there are several significant cities which fringe these fells – places such as Leeds, Bradford, Sheffield, Blackburn, Manchester and Carlisle. Although these cities were once much smaller, man has moved between these places for hundreds of years – originally for trade.

As demand for transport increased, these hills presented engineers with a real challenge, whether that be the first packhorse routes on stone 'causeys' (causeways) or the later turnpike routes around and across the hills. The canal engineers arrived next and faced the challenge by building flights of locks and long tunnels. Next came the railway engineers and they faced the greatest challenge, to find a gradient that was acceptable to adhesion worked trains and burrowing tunnels through hard gritstone and boulder clay. The geology was a serious hindrance to these first railway engineers as the limestone areas held the hidden dangers of sink holes and pot holes which had to be considered when surveying the route. There are also large areas of peat moorland, particularly at higher altitudes which needed careful consideration if they were to provide a firm foundation for a railway. Glacial activity during the ice age carved out some beautiful valleys and dales across which those railway builders built some magnificent viaducts. These graceful structures now seem to blend so well into the landscape that it feels as though they are as natural as the hills and mountains themselves.

These geological features now provide the modern day photographer with a fantastic landscape in which to showcase the steam locomotives that work across these fells. Limestone pavements, gritstone outcrops, high mountains and rolling moorland can all form the foreground or backdrop to a classic image.

The modern day photographer also faces the same challenge as those Victorian railway builders – the weather! The permanent way team on the Settle to Carlisle line will tell you that it is possible to experience four seasons in one day and it is fair to say that this region is often wetter, windier and colder than the lower ground further south and east. That's largely because of the altitude and it being the first point at which the prevailing westerly weather meets this higher ground. A landscape and railway photographer therefore needs a good eye for the weather – firstly to assess whether it's worth venturing out at all – and then to decide on the best place to be. There are many days when I have followed the clouds as they scud across the sky, deciding close to train time whether I need to move to be in with the best chance of sunshine. And then you have to consider the wind – as it can mean the exhaust from the steam train can blow down and obscure the locomotive, the train or the landscape altogether!

Like any landscape photography it pays to do some research and to get to know the area well. Living in North Manchester, the Pennines have always been my playground and I have spent many happy hours walking across most of these hills and through many of these dales. When I am out walking, I often consider the potential of the landscape at different times of day. That is relatively straightforward for traditional landscape photography as the next step is to wait for the requisite weather, turn up at the best time of day and wait for the ideal conditions. You press the shutter and if it isn't quite right, you take another picture, or maybe return the next morning or evening.

When it comes to steam railway photography, the challenge gets that much tougher. Steam trains are so infrequent – perhaps once a week over a certain route – that you have one opportunity to get the shot in a particular location at a specific time of day – and that's if the weather stays good. It can therefore involve hiking over rough ground to a high vantage point to a particular spot that has potential. There are then tense moments of anticipation, waiting for the train, hoping that the sun will continue to shine and there is just one moment, just one chance to get that shot. Once the train has passed, that might be it for another week, another month or maybe even longer!

The usual maxims apply – the best times for steam in the landscape photography are during the autumn and winter months and at the magic hour just after sunrise and just before sunset – but you have to be lucky for that to coincide with the passage of a steam train and for good light. Sometimes it happens though and there is probably more pleasure to be found in that one moment, than if it were easy and you could get the shot without effort.

Regular working steam in this part of England finished in 1968 – the last area for steam to hold out in this country. Today the remaining routes continue to see a number of special steam-hauled charter trains allowing the photographer to witness and capture the spectacle of steam trains working hard against the gradient in magnificent scenery.

A number of Trans Pennine railway routes survive today, including:

The famous **Settle to Carlisle** route which rises from the market town of Settle at the foot of the Yorkshire Dales to carry trains over the 'roof of England', through England's highest main line station – Dent – over the highest point on an English mainline – Ais Gill – and down through the lush Eden Valley to Carlisle. It principally carries passenger trains from Leeds to Carlisle and Anglo-Scottish freight traffic, but it still sees regular steam-hauled excursion trains such as the Fellsman, the Waverley and Cumbrian Mountain Express. There are, therefore, plenty of opportunities for the photographer to get out into the hills and enjoy steam in the landscape.

Carnforth to Skipton. This trans-Pennine route was built principally to connect the port of Barrow and resort at Morecambe with the West Yorkshire towns of Bradford and Leeds, exploiting a natural opening through the Pennines – the Aire Gap – to allow an easier gradient from west to east. Again this route still sees occasional steam traffic and passes along the boundary between the Yorkshire Dales and the Forest of Bowland, an Area of Outstanding Natural Beauty.

Blackburn to Bradford. This trans-Pennine route links the classic mill towns of Lancashire and Yorkshire, including Blackburn, Burnley, Todmorden, Hebden Bridge, Halifax and Bradford. It typically passes through a landscape of mills and gritstone towns and villages, but in between there are some lovely farming landscapes and the route offers a challenge to steam locomotives with its summit at Copy Pit near Todmorden. A series of regular steam hauled specials – the Cotton Mill Express – was a regular feature in these hills until recently.

Bolton to Clitheroe and Hellifield. This route winds through the West Pennine Moors to Blackburn, on through the Ribble Valley and in the shadow of Pendle Hill, to connect with the Settle to Carlisle line at Hellifield. As such it provides an important connection for trains heading to the Settle to Carlisle line and for those Cotton Mill Express trains.

Manchester to Huddersfield and Leeds. Following the line of an earlier trans-Pennine crossing – the Huddersfield Narrow Canal – this route links the principal cities of Lancashire and Yorkshire and is a busy main line on the modern network. It takes the railway through the lovely landscape of Saddleworth and on through Standedge Tunnel to the Yorkshire mill towns beyond. There are regular steam-hauled trains on this route, including the Scarborough Flyer and the Scarborough Spa Express taking daytrippers from North West England to the Yorkshire Coast, much as railways did in their heyday.

Manchester to Sheffield. Again linking two principal cities in Lancashire and Yorkshire, this route passes through the heart of the Peak District National Park and the mecca for all ramblers – Edale and the start of the Pennine Way. Burrowing through two large tunnels at Cowburn and Totley, it passes below Kinder Scout and the famous gritstone edges of this part of the Peak District. Occasional steam excursions still pass this way, including the popular Tin Bath – apparently named in honour of the exploits of the three pensioners in the *Last of the Summer Wine* television series!

Sadly a number of trans-Pennine railway routes were closed, including the Stainmore route from Tebay to Kirkby Stephen and on to County Durham and the famous Woodhead pass – an alternative route from Manchester to Sheffield.

However, railway enthusiasts are working hard to re-open stretches of some of the other Pennine railways, such as the East Lancashire Railway which runs between the West Pennine Moors and Rossendale Fells near Ramsbottom and Rawtenstall; the Wensleydale Railway which links this beautiful Yorkshire dale with the Settle to Carlisle line at Garsdale and the Moorland & City Railway whose line climbs just below the true starting point of the Pennines – the gritstone outcrops of The Roaches.

Chris Gee
Manchester, 2011

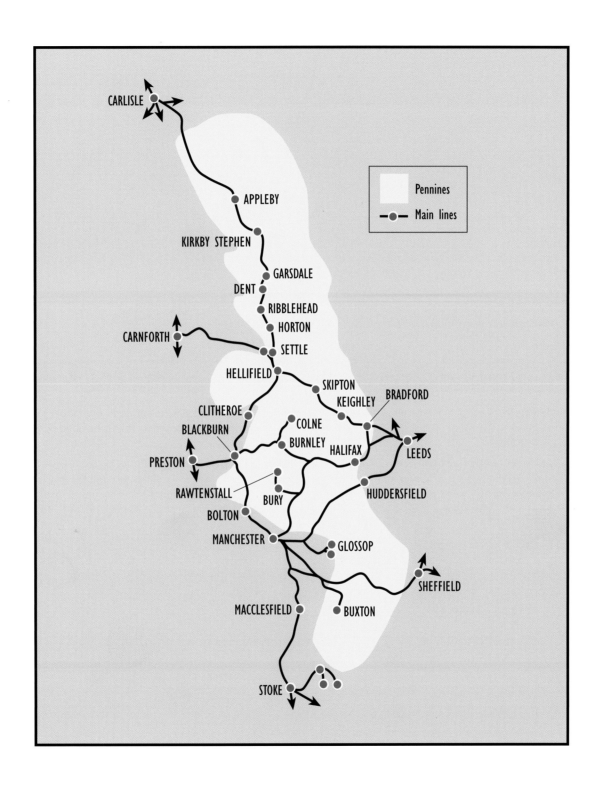

LMS Jubilee class 4-6-0s were a regular form of motive power on the Settle to Carlisle until their withdrawal in 1967. Here LMS-liveried Jubilee No.5690 LEANDER begins the relentless climb up the Long Drag, the dark exhaust indicating that the fireman is already hard at work for the climb to Ais Gill. The train is a northbound Fellsman working on 28 July 2010.

Against a backdrop of the North Pennine fells that includes the full range from Cross Fell to Musgrave Fell, BR Standard 4-6-2 No.71000 DUKE OF GLOUCESTER works hard through Birkett Common on the climb from Kirkby Stephen to the summit of the Settle to Carlisle line at Ais Gill. 3 July 2010.

Anticipation. On a bitterly cold day with a biting north-easterly wind, LMS Jubilee 4-6-0 No.5690 LEANDER climbs through the hamlet of Selside on the Settle to Carlisle line with a northbound Cumbrian Mountain Express on 27 November 2010.

Two turnpike roads dating back to 1759 and the 1790s crossed the Pennines just east of Diggle and were the principal routes through these hills until the Huddersfield Narrow Canal was completed in 1811. The railway arrived soon after and here LMS Princess Royal class 4-6-2 No.6201 PRINCESS ELIZABETH follows the Huddersfield Narrow Canal through Diggle as it climbs towards the summit within Standedge Tunnel. The train is the Scarborough Flyer on 23 July 2010.

The Blackburn to Bolton line cuts through the heart of the West Pennine Moors. Bursting through the castellated bridges at Turton Tower, LMS Royal Scot class 4-6-0 No.46115 SCOTS GUARDSMAN heads towards Bolton with the Cotton Mill Express, a train which links several Pennine towns. 17 July 2010. The castellated bridge was insisted on by the owner of the adjacent fifteenth-century Turton Tower so that the new railway and its infrastructure were in keeping with the rest of his estate.

BR Standard 4-6-2 No.71000 DUKE OF GLOUCESTER is about to leave the lush pastures of the Eden Valley behind as it heads uphill into the wilder moorland terrain towards the summit of the Settle to Carlisle line at Ais Gill. The location is Birkett Common and the train is the southbound Cumbrian Coast Explorer on 3 July 2010.

The flat plains between Settle and Skipton provided a natural break in the high ground of the Pennines and the first roads, canals and then the railway took advantage of this lower lying land to bisect the fells. Here LMS Royal Scot class 4-6-0 No.46115 SCOTS GUARDSMAN races between Settle Junction and Hellifield at Skirbeck with a test train having returned to main line service following repairs. 27 April 2010.

Out on test after repairs at Carnforth, LMS Royal Scot class 4-6-0 No.46115 SCOTS GUARDSMAN passes Starricks Farm near Keerholme on the former trans-Pennine route between Barrow and Skipton. 27 April 2010. This route meanders through the broad Lune Valley towards the Aire Gap – a natural break in the Pennines and an original route of communication between east and west.

LMS Princess Royal Class 4-6-2 No.6201 PRINCESS ELIZABETH works away from Batty Moss with a northbound Cumbrian Mountain Express on 17 April 2010. Batty Moss was the location of an encampment of navvies involved in the construction of the Settle to Carlisle line in the 1870s. Small townships grew up around the route as the line was constructed, with the township at Batty Green home for those navvies building Ribblehead Viaduct.

At the head of a heavy train of thirteen coaches, LMS Royal Scot class 4-6-0 No.46115 SCOTS GUARDSMAN lifts its train up Armathwaite bank at the beginning of the southbound climb over the Settle to Carlisle line. The train is a returning Waverley on 29 August 2010.

Opposite: LMS Class 8F 2-8-0 No.48151 and BR Standard Britannia class 4-6-2 No.70013 OLIVER CROMWELL are well into the climb to Standedge Tunnel as they weave through the reverse curves at Diggle with the Help for Heroes train from Liverpool to York. 27 March 2010.

Armathwaite Bank is one of the first significant climbs on the southbound route over the Settle to Carlisle line and in this image, BR Standard Britannia class 4-6-2 No.70013 OLIVER CROMWELL heads south with a Cumbrian Mountain Express on 29 March 2010.

Winter comes often to the trans-Pennine railway routes and adds texture to the landscape. LMS Black 5 4-6-0 No.45407 leads BR Standard 2-6-0 No.76079 as they climb the final few yards to the summit at Copy Pit between Todmorden and Burnley on 4 March 2006. Black Scout ridge and Whitaker Naze are the snow capped hills above the exhaust.

The fireman lays on some coal for the remaining climb to the summit of the Settle to Carlisle line as LMS Royal Scot class 4-6-0 No.46115 SCOTS GUARDSMAN climbs through Birkett Common with a northbound Waverley on 15 August 2010.

Having taken water at Appleby, the climb up through Ormside is the next big challenge for southbound trains on the Settle to Carlisle line. LNER A1 class 4-6-2 No.60163 TORNADO gets into the climb as it works south at the end of the day on 4 October 2009.

LNER A1 class 4-6-2 No.60163 TORNADO climbs above the rooftops and chimneys of Settle towards Langcliffe with a northbound Waverley on 4 October 2009. This newly constructed locomotive was a welcome addition to main line steam and its first runs over the Settle to Carlisle were eagerly awaited.

On one of its early trips over the Settle to Carlisle line, newly built LNER A1 class 4-6-2 No.60163 TORNADO climbs towards Langcliffe with a northbound Waverley on 4 October 2009.

Heather moorland predominates across much of upland Pennine England, but the heather also creeps down into the rock cuttings driven through these trans-Pennine routes. LMS Princess Royal class 4-6-2 No.6201 PRINCESS ELIZABETH climbs towards Standedge through Quick with an eastbound Scarborough Flyer on 27 August 2010.

At the watershed between the Upper Eden Valley and Upper Wensleydale the Settle to Carlisle line reaches its summit at Ais Gill. LMS Jubilee class 4-6-0 No.5690 LEANDER climbs the final few yards to the summit with the Eden Valley stretching away into the distance. The train is a southbound Fellsman on 9 September 2009. From a point near here, the Eden flows north and west to Carlisle, while the Ure flows south and east to the North Sea.

Getting in some practice for the stiff gradients to come on its journey over the Settle to Carlisle, LMS Jubilee class 4-6-0 No.5690 LEANDER climbs Hoghton Bank with a northbound Fellsman on 9 September 2009. The Fellsman is a name given to a rough fell race that crosses 60 miles of the toughest Pennine terrain. It was also the name chosen for this regular series of days out from Lancaster to Carlisle via the scenic Settle to Carlisle line.

With all its climbing now done for the day, LMS Princess Royal class 4-6-2 No.6201 PRINCESS ELIZABETH brings its train over the last of the banks at Wilpshire with a returning Cumbrian Mountain Express on 22 August 2009. Wilpshire is the last principal gradient on the Ribble Valley route between Hellifield and Blackburn.

The heather is at its best on the Standedge route in the last two weeks of August and here LMS Duchess class 4-6-2 No.6233 DUCHESS OF SUTHERLAND complements the heather with its red livery as it climbs through the cutting at Quick with a Scarborough Flyer on 21 August 2009.

Opposite: Working hard on the climb from Stalybridge to the summit at Standedge on the Manchester to Leeds route, LMS Princess Royal class 4-6-2 No.6201 PRINCESS ELIZABETH works through the gritstone cutting at Quick with an eastbound Scarborough Flyer on 7 August 2009.

The Leeds and Liverpool Canal crossed the Pennines long before the railway did and was the first of the trans-Pennine canals to be started, but the last to be completed, taking 46 years to finish. Here at Gargrave the two modes of transport meet and cross. Holidaymakers on a narrowboat look on as LMS Royal Scot class 4-6-0 No.46115 SCOTS GUARDSMAN passes with a northbound Waverley on 2 August 2009.

Climbing away from a speed restriction at Mossley Station, LMS Duchess class 4-6-2 No.6233 DUCHESS OF SUTHERLAND begins the hard slog up to Standedge with a Scarborough Flyer on 31 July 2009. The Scarborough Flyer trains took daytrippers from North West England to the Yorkshire coastal resort.

The trans Pennine route between Manchester and Leeds climbs relentlessly from Stalybridge to the summit at Standedge and seen early in the climb LMS Black 5 4-6-0 No.45407 is working hard through Quick with a Cotton Mill Express on 26 July 2008.

The landscape around the summit at Copy Pit on the Burnley to Bradford route continues to see a lot of geological movement, resulting in some speed restrictions on the railway. The hillside above Copy Pit holds evidence of previous landslips as LMS Royal Scot class 4-6-0 No.46115 SCOTS GUARDSMAN nears the top with a westbound Cotton Mill Express on 14 July 2009.

LMS Royal Scot class 4-6-0 No.46115 SCOTS GUARDSMAN hauls its heavy train through the reverse curves at Diggle on the climb to Standedge with an eastbound Cotton Mill Express on 14 July 2009.

Ten days earlier and in brighter weather, LMS Princess Royal class 4-6-2 No.6201 PRINCESS ELIZABETH climbs through the same reverse curves at Diggle only this time with a Scarborough Flyer on 4 July 2009.

Against a backdrop of Rye Loaf Hill and the fells above Stockdale, LMS Princess Royal class 4-6-2 No.6201 PRINCESS ELIZABETH works away from Hellifield with a Cumbrian Mountain Express on 23 August 2009.

High above the chimneys and houses of Settle, LMS Jubilee class 4-6-0 No.5690 LEANDER climbs towards Langcliffe with a northbound Fellsman on 25 August 2010. Watershed Mill behind the locomotive was originally built as a cotton mill in 1785 and is now a gift shop and visitor centre.

LMS Black 5 4-6-0 No.45407 is about to breast the summit at Ais Gill on the Settle to Carlisle line while working a southbound Waverley on 8 August 2010. Mallerstang Edge and High Seat dominate the skyline in the background. The railway reaches its summit here at 1,169 feet and this is the highest point on an English mainline.

LMS Duchess class 4-6-2 No.6233 DUCHESS OF SUTHERLAND climbs away from the houses and mills of Settle to begin the long climb through Langcliffe with a northbound Cumbrian Mountain Express on 28 March 2009.

Despite National Park status, large amounts of limestone are still quarried beside the Settle to Carlisle line. LMS Royal Scot class 4-6-0 No.46115 SCOTS GUARDSMAN passes the large Arcow quarry at Helwith Bridge with a northbound Thames-Clyde Express on 7 February 2009.

On a bitterly cold winter's day, LMS Royal Scot class 4-6-0 No.46115 SCOTS GUARDSMAN climbs through Helwith Bridge on the Settle to Carlisle with a northbound Thames-Clyde Express on 7 February 2009. The Thames-Clyde Express was one of the original named trains on this route, operating between London and Glasgow, but ceased running in 1975.

Just beyond the closed station of Saddleworth, LMS Princess Royal class 4-6-2 No.6201 PRINCESS ELIZABETH climbs through the reverse curves to Diggle with a Scarborough Flyer on 4 July 2009. Saddleworth station closed in 1968 with the nearby station at Uppermill now serving the needs of the local passengers.

With twelve coaches on the drawbar, LMS Black 5 4-6-0 No.44932 works hard through the hamlet of Selside with a northbound Waverley on 21 August 2010. Selside is predominantly a sheep-farming hamlet with a cluster of farms and cottages beside the Settle to Ribblehead road.

Long before the real climbing starts on the Settle to Carlisle route, LMS Black 5 4-6-0s No.45407 and No.45231 sprint through the reverse curves at Little Salkeld with a special to mark the 40th anniversary since the end of steam in North West England. 10 August 2008.

Cutting a swathe through the West Pennine Moors, the line between Blackburn and Bolton passes the Elizabethan pele tower at Turton. Threading through the castellated bridges, LMS Jubilee class 4-6-0 No.5690 LEANDER heads south with a Cotton Mill Express on 27 September 2008.

The first testing gradient for the Fellsman trains heading for the Settle to Carlisle line is Hoghton Bank and here LMS Jubilee class 4-6-0 No.5690 LEANDER blackens the sky as it clears the first summit on a largely uphill route. 25 August 2010.

The Lowe and Riddle Scout form the backdrop here for LMS Jubilee class 4-6-0 No.5690 LEANDER as it covers the final few yards to the summit at Copy Pit with a Cotton Mill Express on 27 September 2008.

With the climbing yet to begin, LNER A4 class 4-6-2 No.60009 UNION OF SOUTH AFRICA gets up some speed for the gradients to come on its journey to Standedge with an eastbound Scarborough Flyer on 15 August 2008.

Long before the real climbing starts on the Settle to Carlisle route, LMS Black 5 4-6-0s No.45407 and No.45231 pass Little Salkeld with a special to mark the 40th anniversary since the end of steam in North West England. 10 August 2008.

Just north of Mossley station, LMS Duchess class 4-6-2 No.6233 DUCHESS OF SUTHERLAND begins the long climb up to Standedge with a Scarborough Flyer on 31 July 2009.

To mark the 40th anniversary since the end of steam in North West England, a series of special trains were run to celebrate the occasion. One of the locomotives that operated one of the last of the trains in 1968, BR Standard class 4-6-2 No.70013 OLIVER CROMWELL, is seen here 40 years later climbing through Selside with the northbound special on 10 August 2008.

With a light covering of late winter snow to brighten up the landscape, LMS Royal Scot class 4-6-0 No.46115 SCOTS GUARDSMAN is already working hard up the Long Drag through Helwith Bridge as it climbs the Settle to Carlisle line on a northbound Thames-Clyde Express on 7 February 2009.

Passing the railwaymen's cottages that are found beside the Settle to Carlisle line throughout its length, LMS Black 5 class 4-6-0 No.45407 climbs through the hamlet of Selside with a northbound Waverley on 8 August 2010.

Lush pasture can be found on the valley bottom through Ribblesdale contrasting strongly with the rougher ground on the fells above. Passing the farming community at Selside, LMS Black 5 4-6-0 No.44932 climbs towards Ribblehead with a Waverley excursion on 21 August 2010.

Opposite: Building a railway to cross the Pennines required the construction of both tall viaducts and deep cuttings to maintain a reasonable gradient. LMS Black 5 4-6-0 No.45407 climbs through the gritstone cutting at Quick as it heads to Standedge with a Cotton Mill Express on 26 July 2008.

Struggling on a murky day to bring its train to the top of Wilpshire Bank, BR Standard 2-6-0 No.76079 darkens the sky as it heads north with a Cotton Mill Express on 15 March 2008.

With thirteen coaches in tow, LMS 8F class 2-8-0 No.48151 climbs through Eldroth on the edge of the Yorkshire Dales as it heads for the Aire Gap on 1 March 2008. The Aire Gap was one of the original routes of communication through the Pennines as it formed a natural break in the higher ground.

Bursting from beneath the road bridge that carries the Kirkby Stephen to Garsdale road, LMS Duchess class 4-6-2 No.6233 DUCHESS OF SUTHERLAND approaches the summit at Ais Gill and the county border between Cumbria and Yorkshire with a southbound Cumbrian Mountain Express on 20 August 2010.

On a moody day with brief flashes of sunshine, BR Standard 2-6-0 No.76079 climbs away from Hebden Bridge through Eastwood with a westbound Cotton Mill Express on 12 January 2008.

The closed trans-Pennine route between Garsdale and Northallerton is steadily being reopened in sections by the Wensleydale Railway with the ultimate aim of reinstating the route through to Hawes and eventually Garsdale again. Here BR Standard 2-6-4T No.80105 heads towards Redmire with a westbound service on 26 August 2007.

Getting into its stride before the serious climbing, LNER A4 class 4-6-2 No.60009 UNION OF SOUTH AFRICA sweeps through the reverse curves at Little Salkeld with a southbound Cumbrian Mountain Express on 28 July 2007.

On a balmy summer's day, LMS Princess Royal class 4-6-2 No.6201 PRINCESS ELIZABETH climbs through Langcliffe with the Fishwick Centenarian heading for Carlisle on 28 July 2007.

Semaphore signals still hold sway at the iconic Settle Junction. With the climbing all done, LMS Princess Royal class 4-6-2 No.6201 PRINCESS ELIZABETH gets the road and heads towards Hellifield with an eastbound excursion on 16 June 2007.

With the special train to mark the 40th anniversary since regular steam finished in these hills, LMS Black 5 4-6-0s Nos.45231 and 45407 climb through Birkett Common heading for the summit on 10 August 2008.

Seen from high above Kitson Wood Tunnel, LMS 8F class 2-8-0 No.48151 is about to plunge into the depths of this Pennine tunnel as it climbs to Copy Pit summit with a Cotton Mill Express on 31 January 2009.

LMS Black 5 4-6-0 No.45407 passes beneath the first of two castellated bridges at Turton Tower as it threads its way through the West Pennine Moors between Blackburn and Bolton with a Cotton Mill Express on 28 July 2008.

The arid moorland around Blea Moor indicates a very dry winter and spring – unusual for this part of the Settle to Carlisle line. LMS Princess Royal class 4-6-2 No.6201 PRINCESS ELIZABETH works hard towards Blea Moor Tunnel with a northbound Cumbrian Mountain Express on 17 April 2010.

Surrounded by typical rough grassland and moorland, LMS Jubilee class 4-6-0 No.5690 LEANDER climbs to Ais Gill summit with a southbound Fellsman on 9 September 2009.

With the fireman putting another shovelful of coal on the fire, LMS Royal Scot class 4-6-0 No.46115 SCOTS GUARDSMAN continues the long climb through Birkett Common towards the summit of the Settle to Carlisle at Ais Gill with a southbound Waverley on 15 August 2010.

Beneath brooding skies and dark fells, LMS 8F class 2-8-0 No.48151 hurries across Stonehouse Brow on the lower flanks of Great Knoutberry Hill with a southbound Fellsman on 18 August 2010.

Stonehouse Brow carries the Settle to Carlisle line on a shelf below the lower flanks of Great Knoutberry Hill. Here LMS Black 5 4-6-0 No.45407 works between Dent and Arten Gill with a southbound Waverley on 22 August 2010. The revived Waverley excursions recall the named train that used to operate over this route between London St Pancras and Edinburgh Waverley, but which finished running in 1968.

In a typical North Pennine landscape of livestock pasture, drystone walls, field barns and moorland, LMS Jubilee class 4-6-0 No.5690 LEANDER climbs the final few yards to the summit at Ais Gill with a southbound Fellsman on 1 September 2010.

Beneath Little Whernside, LMS Jubilee class 4-6-0 No.5690 LEANDER heads across Blea Moor with a northbound Cumbrian Mountain Express on 17 October 2009. It is about to pass Blea Moor signalbox, one of the loneliest signalling outposts in England.

Battling hard against a north-easterly wind, LMS Jubilee class 4-6-0 No.5690 LEANDER works hard through Selside with a northbound Cumbrian Mountain Express on 27 November 2010. Winter came early to the Three Peaks area of the Yorkshire Dales with a blanket of snow on Penyghent and temperatures well below freezing.

Pendle Hill is a Pennine outlier – formed largely of typical Pennine gritstone. In temperatures well below zero, LMS Jubilee class 4-6-0 No.5690 LEANDER disturbs the frost on the rails as it heads north through Newsholme to Hellifield to begin the long climb of the Settle to Carlisle with a Cumbrian Mountain Express. 27 November 2010.

With the distinctive Rye Loaf Hill on the horizon, BR Standard 4-6-2 No.71000 DUKE OF GLOUCESTER gets into its stride as it pulls away from Hellifield at Hellifield Green with the Cumbrian Coast Explorer on 3 July 2010.

Against a backdrop of the West Pennine Moors with Musbury Tor prominent, BR Standard 4-6-2 No.71000 DUKE OF GLOUCESTER lays a trail of white exhaust as it pulls away from Irwell Vale while working between two classic Pennine towns – Ramsbottom and Rawtenstall. 24 October 2010.

The exhaust almost obliterates Pendle Hill as LMS Jubilee class 4-6-0 No.5690 LEANDER works hard up Rimington Bank with a Fellsman train heading for Carlisle on 1 September 2010. The bulk of Pendle Hill belies its stature as at 1,827 feet it falls short of mountain status.

Opposite: The West Pennine Moors with Bull Hill and Holcombe Moor dominate this scene at Irwell Vale on the East Lancashire Railway as BR Standard 4-6-2 No.71000 DUKE OF GLOUCESTER departs with a train for Rawtenstall. 24 October 2010.

LNER A1 class 4-6-2 No.60163 TORNADO blows its whistle and starts to work its train away from Hellifield at Hellifield Green with the southbound Border Raider on 24 June 2010. The prominent peak on the skyline is Rye Loaf Hill.

The highest of Yorkshire's Three Peaks – Whernside – dominates this scene at Ribblehead station as LNER A1 class 4-6-2 No.60163 TORNADO drifts through the station with the southbound Border Raider on 24 June 2010.

The 24 arches of Ribblehead Viaduct are a magnificent engineering achievement, but are dwarfed by the bulk of Whernside (2,415 feet) in this image of LNER A4 class 4-6-2 No.60019 BITTERN drifting downhill into Ribblehead station on 20 May 2010.

Opposite: The Three Peaks dominate the southern half of the Settle to Carlisle line and here Penyghent towers above Ribblehead Viaduct as LMS Princess Royal Class 4-6-2 No.6201 PRINCESS ELIZABETH heads north with a Cumbrian Mountain Express on 17 April 2010.

Penyghent overlooks the popular village of Horton-in-Ribblesdale and starting point of the famous Three Peaks Walk. Here LMS Jubilee class 4-6-0 No.5690 LEANDER passes above the village with a southbound Fellsman on 28 July 2010. At 2,277 feet, Penyghent is the smallest of the Three Peaks, but one of the most distinctive and often described as like a sleeping lion.

Ingleborough and Simon Fell form a backdrop to this scene as LMS Jubilee class 4-6-0 No.5690 LEANDER works off Ribblehead Viaduct with a northbound Cumbrian Mountain Express on 17 October 2009. At 2,372 feet, Ingleborough is the last in the trio of peaks that feature in the classic Three Peaks Walk.

The highest peak on the Pennines – Cross Fell – at 2,930 feet dominates this scene at Keld, north of Appleby. LMS Royal Scot class 4-6-0 No.46115 SCOTS GUARDSMAN shuts off for a water stop as it heads south with the Waverley on 15 August 2010.

Rain clouds gather over Rye Loaf Hill as the last of the sun catches LMS 8F class 2-8-0 No.48151 as it departs Hellifield with a south-bound Fellsman on 18 August 2010.

With Pendle Hill on the skyline, LMS Black 5 4-6-0 No.45231 climbs Rimington Bank with a northbound Fellsman on 23 September 2009.

LMS Jubilee class 4-6-0 No.5690 LEANDER works away from Hellifield on a glorious summer's evening with a southbound Fellsman on 9 September 2009 obliterating Rye Loaf Hill with its exhaust.

Opposite: The lower flanks of Wild Boar Fell merge into High Bank above Mallerstang. The railway runs along a shelf below High Bank and above the Upper Eden Valley. Here LMS Jubilee class 4-6-0 No.5690 LEANDER draws its train from below Wild Boar Fell to the summit at Ais Gill on 9 September 2009 with a southbound Fellsman.

Penyghent has watched over the Settle to Carlisle line since its opening in 1875, witnessing both the end of steam and the return of steam on these fells. Here BR Standard class 4-6-2 No.70013 OLIVER CROMWELL climbs through Selside with a northbound special on 10 August 2008.

Against a backdrop of Rye Loaf Hill and the fells above Stockdale, LMS Princess Royal class 4-6-2 No.6201 PRINCESS ELIZABETH works away from Hellifield with a Cumbrian Mountain Express on 23 August 2009.

Working away from Hellifield, LMS Royal Scot class 4-6-0 No.46115 SCOTS GUARDSMAN heads south with a returning Fellsman on 5 August 2009.

Wild Boar Fell watches over the classic railway location at Ais Gill as LMS Royal Scot class 4-6-0 No.46115 SCOTS GUARDSMAN climbs the final few yards to the summit. The train is the southbound Fellsman on 5 August 2009.

Mallerstang Edge and Hangingstone Scar dominate the skyline as LMS Black 5 4-6-0 No.45407 approaches the summit and Yorkshire/Cumbria county border at Ais Gill with a southbound Waverley on 8 August 2010.

Having emerged from Cowburn Tunnel which burrows deep beneath the Pennines, BR Standard 2-6-0 No.76079 and LMS Black 5 4-6-0 No.45407 pass through Barber Booth with a Tin Bath excursion on 29 March 2009. The hill in the background is Brown Knoll and forms part of a popular horseshoe walk from Lose Hill to Mam Tor to Kinder Scout.

Opposite: Edale and where most people think the Pennines begin. Just about to pass Edale signalbox, BR Standard 2-6-0 No.76079 and LMS Black 5 4-6-0 No.45407 hurry along the Hope Valley with a Tin Bath excursion on 29 March 2009. The gritstone plateau on the skyline is Stanage Edge – popular rock climbing territory and Edale is the official start of the classic Pennine Way walk to the Scottish border at Kirk Yetholm. The true geological start of the Pennines is further south in Staffordshire.

Penyghent is one of the most iconic Yorkshire fells and one of the Three Peaks covered on the famous circular walk. Here it watches over LMS Black 5 4-6-0 No.44932 as it climbs through Selside with a northbound Waverley on 21 August 2010.

Smearsett Scar is a classic limestone outcrop high above Ribblesdale and here it is seen in the background as LNER A4 class 4-6-2 No.60007 SIR NIGEL GRESLEY races through Helwith Bridge on a blustery day with a northbound Cumbrian Mountain Express on 1 November 2008.

On a warm early autumn afternoon, LMS Jubilee class 4-6-0 No.5690 LEANDER climbs beneath Black Scout heading for the summit at Copy Pit with a Cotton Mill Express on 27 September 2008.

Penyghent is shrouded in rain beneath a storm cloud as LMS Royal Scot class 4-6-0 No.46115 SCOTS GUARDSMAN battles uphill with a Thames-Clyde Express on 16 August 2008 – almost 40 years to the day since regular steam finished in the Pennines.

In typical wet Pennine summer weather, BR Standard 4-6-2 No.70013 OLIVER CROMWELL climbs through Rimington, the exhaust almost hiding Pendle Hill behind. The train is a 40th anniversary special to mark the end of steam on British Railways. 10 August 2008.

Opposite: The Upper Eden Valley and Mallerstang Common form the backdrop to this image of LMS Black 5 4-6-0 No.45407 as it approaches the summit at Ais Gill with a southbound Waverley on 8 August 2010.

The highest of the Three Peaks – Whernside – fills the sky above LMS 8F class 2-8-0 No.48151 as it approaches Ribblehead station with a southbound Dalesman excursion on 23 July 2008.

Ingleborough is seen under leaden skies as LMS 8F class 2-8-0 No.48151 climbs through Kettlesbeck heading for York via the Aire Gap on 1 March 2008.

Restarting its train after slipping to a stand on the wet rails, BR Standard 2-6-0 No.76079 gets to grips with the climb to Copy Pit with a Cotton Mill Express on 12 January 2008. Black Scout is the ridge on the skyline.

Wild Boar Fell towers over this scene at Ais Gill Summit as LNER A4 class 4-6-2 No.60009 UNION OF SOUTH AFRICA effortlessly brings its train over the head of the Upper Eden Valley. The train is a southbound Cumbrian Mountain Express on 28 July 2007.

Even at the foot of the Settle to Carlisle line, Penyghent can still be seen top right in this image of LMS Princess Royal class 4-6-2 No.6201 PRINCESS ELIZABETH as it approaches Settle Junction with an eastbound excursion on 16 June 2007.

Opposite: Almost insignificant amongst the glacial landscape around Mallerstang Common, LMS Jubilee class 4-6-0 No.5690 LEANDER makes itself seen and heard as it heads along Mallerstang with a southbound Fellsman on 1 September 2010.

Mallerstang Edge, High Seat and Hangingstone Scar form the backdrop to this image of LMS Jubilee class 4-6-0 No.5690 LEANDER as it heads south with a Fellsman on 1 September 2010.

This is where the Pennines really begin – the gritstone outcrop of the Roaches and the peak of Shutlingsloe are the geological southernmost tip of this 'backbone of England'. Here LMS Black 5 4-6-0 No.44767 GEORGE STEPHENSON climbs towards Ipstones Summit on the Moorland & City Railway, heading for the terminus at Cauldon Low. 13 November 2010.

The Pennine mill town of Hebden Bridge retains much of its character from an earlier time and this is equally true of the station which has kept its old name boards and station signs. LMS Princess Royal Class 4-6-2 No.6201 PRINCESS ELIZABETH passes through the staggered platforms with a train from Liverpool to York on 13 December 2009.

Opposite: Running across the roof of England, LMS Black 5 4-6-0 No.44932 hurries away from Dent station – the highest mainline station in England – across Stonehouse Brow with a southbound Waverley excursion on 21 August 2010. This section of the Settle to Carlisle line was regularly blocked by snowdrifts and the remains of the now redundant snow fences can still be seen today. Baugh Fell is the huge fell in the background that dwarfs the train.

This pair of LMS Black 5 4-6-0s No.45407 and 45231 are about to plunge into the three-and-a-half mile Totley Tunnel that bores beneath the Pennines. The pair are just passing Grindleford signalbox and about to pass through the station with the Tin Bath excursion on 23 October 2009.

The regulars in the Station Inn at Ribblehead will be distracted from their pints as LMS Jubilee class 4-6-0 No.5690 LEANDER works away from Ribblehead station with a northbound Cumbrian Mountain Express on 17 October 2009. The path in the foreground is part of the famous Three Peaks route and a party of walkers is already setting off for Whernside.

Watched over by a group of ramblers about to set off for Ingleborough, LMS Jubilee class 4-6-0 No.5690 LEANDER thunders through Horton-in-Ribblesdale station with a Settle to Carlisle express on 17 May 2009.

A deserted and typically wet Horton-in-Ribblesdale station plays host to LMS Black 5 No.45231 climbing north with the Waverley on 22 August 2009.

Much to the delight of waiting passengers, LMS Royal Scot class 4-6-0 No.46115 SCOTS GUARDSMAN roars through Horton-in-Ribblesdale with a northbound Waverley on 2 September 2008.

Awaiting the road... The crew of LMS Royal Scot class 4-6-0 No.46115 SCOTS GUARDSMAN wait patiently at Hellifield with a northbound Thames-Clyde Express on 7 February 2009. Hellifield is the regular changeover point from diesel to steam for trains about to take on the challenge of the Settle to Carlisle line.

Having filled its tender with water at Hellifield, the signal is cleared to allow LNER A4 class 4-6-2 No.60007 SIR NIGEL GRESLEY to shunt onto the front of the Cumbrian Mountain Express before taking it north over the Settle to Carlisle on 1 November 2008.

The hard work all done, LMS Black 5 class 4-6-0 hurries away from Hellifield heading towards the Aire Gap and York with a Waverley excursion on 21 August 2010.

Passing the closed station at Saddleworth, LMS Black 5 class 4-6-0 No.45407 climbs towards the summit at Standedge with a Cotton Mill Express on 18 May 2008. The station closed 40 years earlier in 1968 and is now a private residence.

LMS Princess Royal Class 4-6-2 No.6201 PRINCESS ELIZABETH waits to take water at Hellifield having worked the Cumbrian Mountain Express across the Settle to Carlisle line. 16 June 2007.

Waiting to go the other way, LMS Duchess class 4-6-2 No.6233 DUCHESS OF SUTHERLAND sits in the loop and waits for its train to arrive at Hellifield before taking it north across the Settle to Carlisle line on 28 March 2009.

Opposite: Horton-in-Ribblesdale station plays host to LMS Jubilee class 4-6-0 No.5690 LEANDER as it climbs on its way north with a Settle to Carlisle Express on 17 May 2009.

Many of the stations on the Settle to Carlisle line are lovingly restored with great attention to period detail. With the hard work all done, LMS 8F class 2-8-0 No.48151 drifts downhill through Garsdale station with a southbound Waverley excursion on 25 July 2010. The brooding hillside in the background is Tarn Hill, part of Abbotside Common.

Freight engines working passenger trains were not altogether uncommon during the steam era on the Settle to Carlisle line and here LMS class 8F 2-8-0 No.48151 works hard to lift its thirteen coach train the final mile to the summit at Ais Gill. It is seen crossing Lunds Viaduct just north of Garsdale with a northbound Waverley on 25 July 2010 against a backdrop of Widdale Fell.

August Bank Holiday weekend on the Settle to Carlisle and not untypical weather – cold, wet and windy! BR Standard 4-6-2 No.70013 OLIVER CROMWELL crosses Ribblehead Viaduct on 30 August 2009 with a northbound Cumbrian Mountain Express.

The Pennine Way follows the high ground across Round Hill and Black Moss seen on the skyline of this photograph as LMS Princess Royal class 4-6-2 No.6201 PRINCESS ELIZABETH drifts across Saddleworth Viaduct on the route between Leeds and Manchester. The train is the return leg of a Scarborough Flyer on 23 July 2010 and the Saddleworth Viaduct carries the railway over both the River Tame and the Huddersfield Narrow Canal.

Crossing the River Calder on the impressive Whalley Viaduct, BR Standard 4-6-2 No.71000 DUKE OF GLOUCESTER works a southbound Cumbrian Coast Explorer towards Blackburn on 3 July 2010.

The magnificent brick arch Whalley Viaduct carries the railway high across the River Calder between Blackburn and Clitheroe. Here LNER A1 class 4-6-2 No.60163 TORNADO enjoys the last of the summer light as it heads south with the Border Raider on 24 June 2010.

Right: Crossing the River Calder on Whalley Viaduct, LNER A1 class 4-6-2 No.60163 TORNADO works the Border Raider south towards Blackburn on 24 June 2010. With 48 arches, the viaduct is the longest in Lancashire and at the time of construction between 1846 and 1850 had its own brickworks on site.

The graceful arches of Ribblehead Viaduct complement this scene of Ribblesdale with Ingleborough dominant and the characteristic limestone pavements of Runscar Scar in the foreground. LMS Jubilee class 4-6-0 No.5690 LEANDER works across the viaduct with a northbound Fellsman train on 1 September 2010.

The sun sets over the River Calder as LMS class 8F 2-8-0 No.48151 works south across Whalley Viaduct with a returning Fellsman on 18 August 2010. The viaduct is locally known as 'Whalley Arches'.

Although Ribblehead Viaduct carries the railway across the head of the dale, it doesn't actually span the River Ribble. LMS Princess Royal Class 4-6-2 No.6201 PRINCESS ELIZABETH battles against a strong westerly wind as it heads north with a Cumbrian Mountain Express on 17 April 2010.

A light load for a Gresley Pacific. LNER A4 class 4-6-2 No.60019 BITTERN drifts across Saddleworth Viaduct and through the closed Saddleworth station with its support coach working back to York after bringing a charter from London to the North West. 27 March 2010.

The tall Smardale Viaduct is one of two viaducts built on separate lines to cross the deep valley through which Scandal Beck flows. LMS Royal Scot class 4-6-0 No.46115 SCOTS GUARDSMAN crosses the Settle to Carlisle structure against a background of High Pike Hill and High Seat. The other viaduct is now disused, but carries a footpath along the route of the former line between Tebay and Kirkby Stephen. 29 August 2010.

Arten Gill Viaduct is a massive structure built to carry the Settle to Carlisle line over the deep cleft of Arten Gill, although the beck itself seen in the foreground is not a significant watercourse. Towards the end of the day, LMS Royal Scot class 4-6-0 No.46115 SCOTS GUARDSMAN crosses the viaduct with a southbound Waverley on 29 August 2010.

LMS Royal Scot class 4-6-0 No.46115 SCOTS GUARDSMAN races across Capernwray Viaduct on the former transpennine route between Barrow and Skipton with an empty coaching stock train for Ely in Cambridgeshire. 21 March 2009.

Working slowly, but surely across the magnificent Ribblehead Viaduct, LMS Jubilee class 4-6-0 No.5690 LEANDER heads north with a Cumbrian Mountain Express on 17 October 2009. Park Fell towers over both train and viaduct.

Against the setting sun, LNER A1 class 4-6-2 No.60163 TORNADO works across Ormside Viaduct with a southbound Waverley on 4 October 2009. The viaduct carries the railway over the infant River Eden.

The sun had already set as LMS Princess Royal class 4-6-2 No.6201 PRINCESS ELIZABETH disturbs the peace while crossing over Slaithwaite Viaduct with the returning Scarborough Flyer on 27 August 2010.

Just after sunset, LMS Jubilee class 4-6-0 No.5690 LEANDER crosses Whalley Viaduct with a returning Fellsman on 9 September 2009.

If ever a fell were so inappropriately named – Little Whernside towers over Ribblehead Viaduct as LMS Black 5 4-6-0 No.44932 heads north with a Waverley excursion on 21 August 2010.

Crossing the River Calder on Whalley Viaduct, LMS Royal Scot 4-6-0 No.46115 SCOTS GUARDSMAN heads south with a returning Fellsman on 5 August 2009.

Seen from Runscar Scar, LMS Royal Scot class 4-6-0 No.46115 SCOTS GUARDSMAN drifts across Ribblehead Viaduct against a backdrop of Little Whernside with a southbound Waverley on 2 August 2009.

LMS Black 5 4-6-0 No.45407 crosses the large arch on Saddleworth Viaduct that spans the Huddersfield Narrow Canal down in the valley below. The locomotive is returning with its support coach from York to Bury on 31 July 2009.

In typical upland Dales scenery of field barns and drystone walls, LMS 8F class 2-8-0 No.48151 is briefly illuminated as it steps onto Arten Gill Viaduct with a southbound Fellsman on 18 August 2010.

Seen from the gatehouse of Whalley Abbey, LMS Jubilee class 4-6-0 No.5690 LEANDER crosses Whalley Viaduct with a southbound Fellsman on 28 July 2010. This fourteenth century gatehouse forms part of the adjacent Cistercian Whalley Abbey.

Saddleworth Viaduct carries the Manchester to Leeds route high above the River Tame, the village of Uppermill and the Huddersfield Narrow Canal. LMS 8F class 2-8-0 No.48151 is silhouetted against a wintry sky as it works towards Standedge with a Cotton Mill Express on 31 January 2009.

Crossing Arten Gill Viaduct and the deep ghyll below, LMS Black 5 4-6-0 No.44932 heads south with a Waverley service on 21 August 2010.

LMS Black 5 4-6-0 No.45407 emerges from Kitson Wood Tunnel to cross Lydgate Viaduct as it climbs towards Copy Pit with a Cotton Mill Express on 26 July 2008. This valley continues to see geological movement – note the distortion of the viaduct beneath the fourth coach, necessitating a speed restriction on this section.

Church Viaduct carries the railway above the rooftops of Settle and here LMS 8F class 2-8-0 No.48151 climbs away from the market town with a northbound Dalesman on 24 May 2008. Settle parish church appropriately overlooks the viaduct.

Ais Gill Viaduct is a short viaduct that carries the railway over the deep ghyll beneath. LMS Jubilee class 4-6-0 No.5690 LEANDER heads south with a Fellsman on 1 September 2010.

A practically monochrome image of BR Standard 2-6-0 No.76079 crossing Wayoh Viaduct above one of the three reservoirs that nestle in this area of the West Pennine Moors. The train is a Cotton Mill Express heading south for Bolton on 12 January 2008.

LMS 8F class 2-8-0 No.48151 works across Whalley Viaduct at the close of day with a southbound Fellsman on 18 August 2010.

On a glorious summer's evening, LMS Princess Royal class 4-6-2 No.6201 PRINCESS ELIZABETH drifts across Saddleworth Viaduct on the route between Leeds and Manchester. The train is the return leg of a Scarborough Flyer on 23 July 2010 and there are about ten minutes to go before the sun sets behind the fells in the west. Broadstone Hill is the fell high above the Saddleworth town of Uppermill.

The short Gisburn Tunnel is castellated to complement the adjacent Gisburne Park and was insisted upon by the owner Lord Ribblesdale when the railway was first constructed here. The tunnel carries the railway beneath its grounds. LMS Jubilee class 4-6-0 No.5690 LEANDER emerges from its confines with a southbound Fellsman on 28 July 2010.

With LMS Princess Royal Class 4-6-2 No.6201 PRINCESS ELIZABETH in charge, this Scarborough Flyer is about to plunge into the three mile long Standedge Tunnel which will carry the railway deep beneath the Pennine hill after which the tunnel takes its name. At the same time the train will cross from Lancashire into Yorkshire. 23 July 2010.

New Brighton Viaduct at Gargrave carries the railway over the River Aire. The low lying ground through the Aire Valley has long been a natural route for communication and transport and was a natural choice for the railway surveyors. Not long after leaving Skipton, LNER A1 class 4-6-2 No.60163 TORNADO passes with a Waverley train for Carlisle. 4 October 2009.

Climbing hard towards Horton-in-Ribblesdale, LMS Black 5 4-6-0 No.45231 hauls a Fellsman train up the Long Drag bound for Carlisle. The railway engineers built the Settle-Carlisle with a prevailing gradient of 1:100 to allow trains to maintain a reasonable speed when climbing the hills. 23 September 2009.

On a warm day of heavy summer rain and almost tropical conditions in the woods, LMS Royal Scot class 4-6-0 No.46115 SCOTS GUARDSMAN is about to plunge into Kitson Wood Tunnel near Todmorden with a Cotton Mill Express on 4th July 2010.

With the heather starting to fade as summer heads towards autumn, LMS Princess Royal class 4-6-2 No.6201 PRINCESS ELIZABETH climbs away from Mossley with an eastbound Scarborough Flyer. It would be a wet day for those travelling to the seaside. 4 September 2009.

Against a backdrop of Flasby Fell, LMS Royal Scot class 4-6-0 No.46115 SCOTS GUARDSMAN crosses the River Aire on New Brighton Viaduct at Gargrave. The train is a northbound Waverley that has just left Skipton and is bound for Carlisle. 2 August 2009.